WHEELS
MAKE THE WORLD GO ROUND

SIMPLE MACHINES
FOR KIDS

Andi Diehn

Illustrated by Micah Rauch

EXPLORE THE BIOMES IN THIS PICTURE BOOK SCIENCE SET!

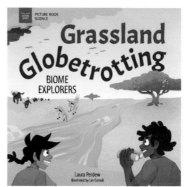

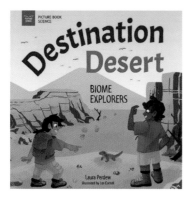

Check out more titles at www.nomadpress.net

Nomad Press

A division of Nomad Communications

10 9 8 7 6 5 4 3 2

This book was manufactured by CGB Printers,
North Mankato, Minnesota, United States

ISBN Softcover: 978-1-64741-110-7
ISBN Hardcover: 978-1-64741-107-7

Educational Consultant, Marla Conn

Questions regarding the ordering of this book should be addressed to
Nomad Press
PO Box 1036, Norwich, VT 05055
www.nomadpress.net

Printed in the United States.

Fight against friction—
With wheels!

Wagons, bikes, roller skates,
and wheelbarrows

**All use wheels to get from here
to there and back to here.**

Potter's wheels:
important for
making art!

**Waterwheels:
important for doing
work before electricity!**

And a Ferris wheel:
important for having
fun at the county fair!

If you were designing a **wheelbarrow,**
how would you make it move
so you could *easily push it?*

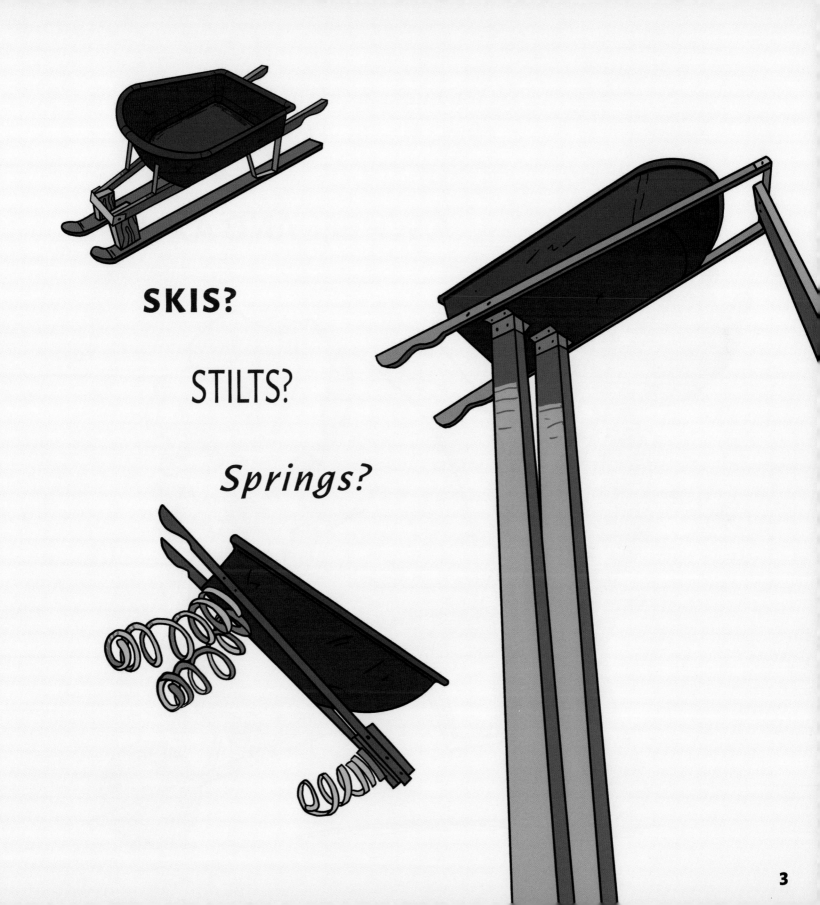

SKIS?

STILTS?

Springs?

You might decide to use the same thing people have used for **thousands of years**:

A WHEEL AND AXLE!

A wheel and axle is a **simple machine.**

Simple machines are devices that make it easier for us to do work. **How?**

By giving us a **mechanical advantage.**

A mechanical advantage makes your pushing and pulling force much more powerful than when you use only your own muscles.

There are **two parts** to a wheel and axle.

The **round wheel** part lets it <u>roll along the ground easily</u>. **What would happen if wheels were square?**

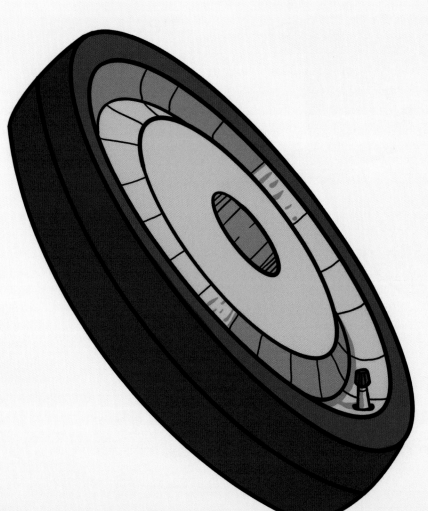

Think of something with wheels, such as a scooter, and imagine how **square wheels** would feel!

Other simple machines include inclined planes, levers, wedges, pulleys, and screws.

The other part is the **axle.** The **axle** is the ROD that goes ~~THROUGH THE CENTER~~ of the **wheel** and stays in place while the wheel moves around it.

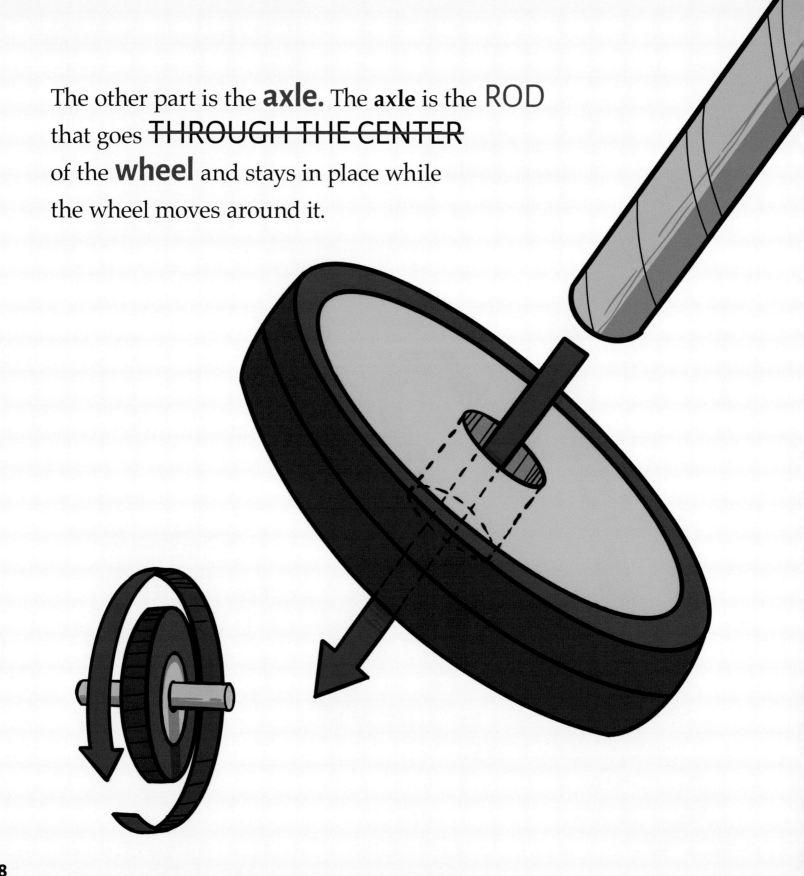

The **axle** is also attached to whatever the wheel is part of—car, bike, or train.

Without an axle, the wheel would simply bounce away down the road—**not useful to anyone!**

Imagine pushing a wheelbarrow
that has SKIS instead of a **WHEEL.**

That might be pretty fun if there's snow
on the ground, but if you have to

PUSH THE WHEELBARROW
over **dirt**
or **pebbles,** the skis
won't work very well.

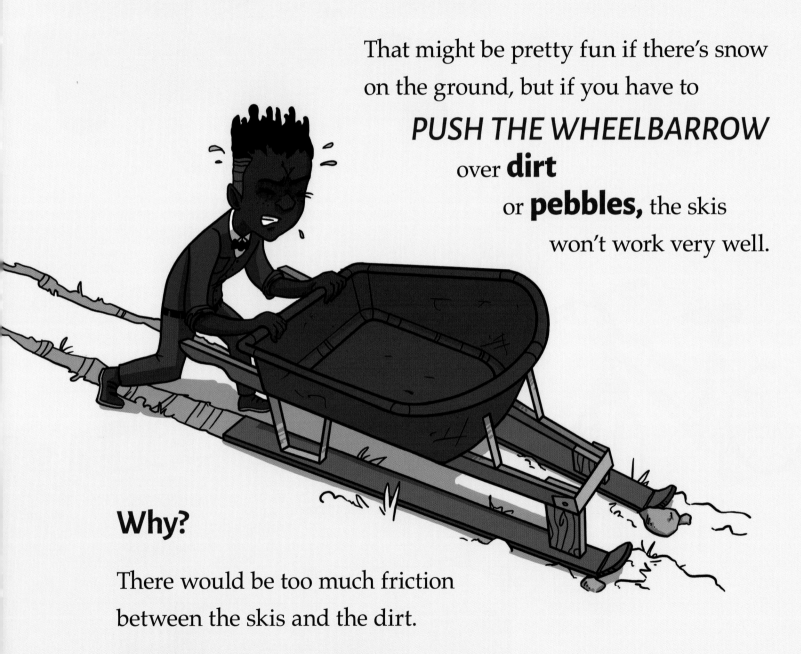

Why?

There would be too much friction
between the skis and the dirt.

Friction is a type of *force.*

And the **HEAVIER THE STUFF** you put in your wheelbarrow, the <u>MORE FRICTION</u> there would be.

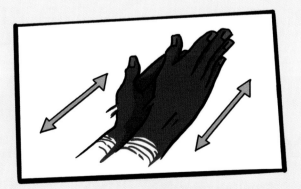

Rub your hands together back and forth very quickly! What do you feel? That's friction!

But replace those <u>SKIS</u> with a **WHEEL** and you can *push the wheelbarrow* pretty easily.

When you LIFT the handles and *push*, the wheel rolls along the ground with FAR LESS **friction** to push against.

Where else can you find a **wheel and axle?**
Think about how you make a bicycle move.

You **push** on the **pedals.**
Those <u>**pedals are connected to a chain,**</u>
and that <u>**chain is connected to the wheels.**</u>

When you **push** on the **pedals** of a bike, that **force** **s p r e a d s** outward to the edges of the **wheels,** making the wheels *roll along the ground.*

Because **axles** attach the **wheels** to your bike, the <u>**whole bike follows the wheels**</u> and *moves as one down the road.*

What about the **wheels** on a car, truck, or bus?
These work in the same way as the bike, but instead of
us *powering* them with our feet, we have
engines to *provide the power* for us.

Because pedaling a car would be
A LOT OF WORK!

Humans have been using wheels and axles for **thousands of years.**

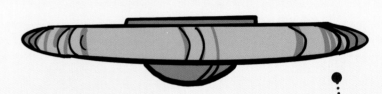

The very first **wheels** weren't used for transportation at all.

They were pottery wheels!

A potter puts a mound of clay on a pottery wheel and, as the **wheel moves,** the potter can mold the clay into whatever they like—a bowl, a vase, or a cup.

Wheels began to appear on **carts** in societies in western Asia about 6,000 years ago. These wheels were **SOLID** and **HEAVY.**

Then, about 4,000 years ago, people got the idea of HOLLOWING out the **wheel** so it would be LIGHTER and even *easier to move* on its axle.

Now, wheels are designed to work best at
whatever job they are meant to do.

Spiked wheels help vehicles *move through snow* or
mud. THIN WHEELS can make a road bike *speedy,* since
there's less friction between the wheel and the road.

Have you ever seen a picture of a waterwheel?

That's a **GIANT WHEEL** set in a river.
The water *moved the wheel,* and
that **force** was used to do different kinds
of work, such as <u>grind wheat</u>.

Before electricity, people used
waterwheels for all kinds of work.

Today, we can see **wheels and axles** performing <u>**many different jobs**</u>,

Such as making a **Ferris wheel spin**

or moving an **electric fan.**

You might even have a wheel in your kitchen drawer—a **pizza cutter!**

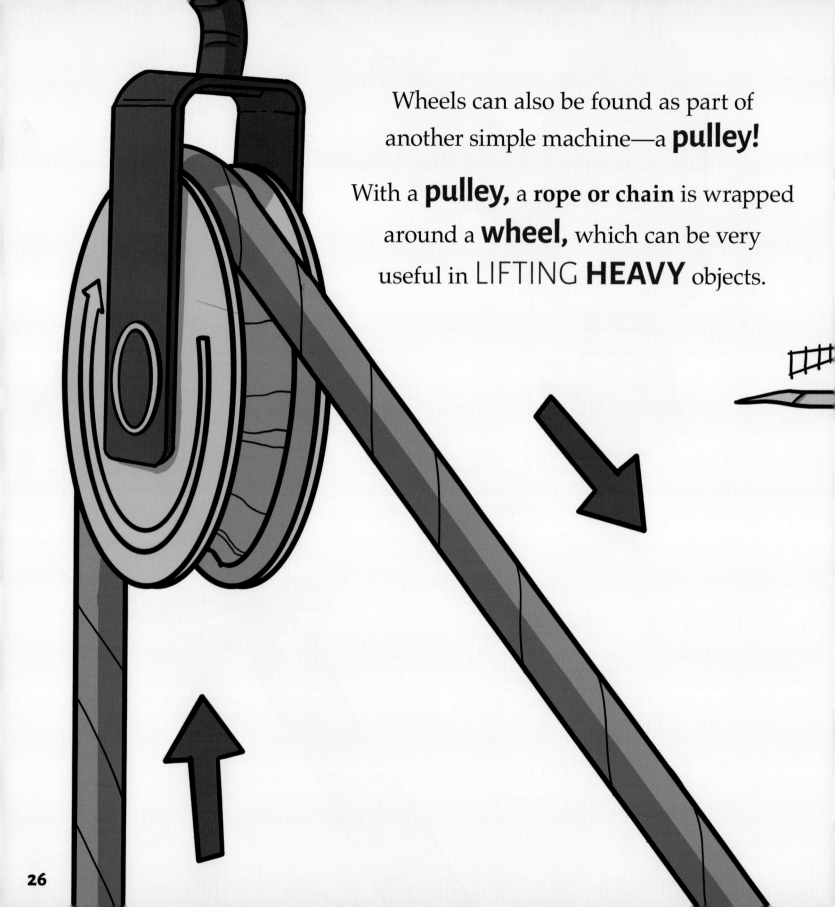

Wheels can also be found as part of another simple machine—a **pulley!**

With a **pulley,** a **rope or chain** is wrapped around a **wheel,** which can be very useful in LIFTING **HEAVY** objects.

Look around your neighborhood.

Where do you spot wheels?

Waterwheel!

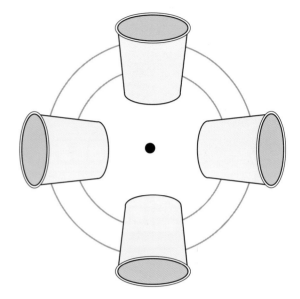

What You Need

a sturdy straw - two paper plates - four paper cups - tape

What You Do

- Poke holes through the center of each paper plate.

- Tape the paper cups on one of the plates so the openings point out in four different directions. Leave the hole open in the middle.

- Tape the other plate to the other side of the cups, so it looks like a sandwich with the cups in the middle.

- Thread the straw through the holes.

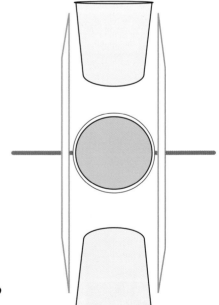

Try It! Holding onto each side of the straw, hold your waterwheel under running water. What happens? What force is moving your waterwheel?

Glossary

axle: a rod on which a wheel rotates.

force: a push or pull that changes an object's motion.

friction: a force that slows down objects when they rub against each other.

inclined plane: a sloped surface that connects a lower level to a higher level.

lever: a bar that rests on a support and lifts or moves things.

load: an applied force or weight.

mechanical advantage: the amount a machine increases or changes a force to make a task easier.

pulley: a wheel with a grooved rim that a rope or chain is pulled through to help lift a load.

screw: an inclined plane wrapped around a central axis used to lift objects or hold things together.

simple machine: a device that changes the direction or strength of a force. The six simple machines are the inclined plane, lever, pulley, screw, wedge, and wheel and axle.

wedge: a simple machine that is thick at one end and narrow at the other. It is used for splitting, tightening, and securing objects.

wheel: a circular object that revolves on an axle and is fixed below a vehicle or other object to make it move easily over the ground.

wheel and axle: a wheel with a rod that turn together to lift and move loads.

work: the force applied to an object to move it across a distance.

Inclined Plane

Wedge

Lever

SIMPLE MACHINES

Pulley

Screw

Wheel and Axle